AWAKENING INNER PEACE

First published in 2018 by Columba Books
23 Merrion Square
Dublin 2
Ireland
www.columbabooks.com

ISBN: 978-1-78218-344-0
Set in Tisa Pro 9/14 and Essonnes Display
Book design by Alba Esteban | Columba Books
Printed with Jellyfish Solutions

Awakening Inner Peace

A LITTLE BOOK *of* HOURS

SISTER STAN

CONTENTS

Introduction

This book is for everyone. It a journey through the hours of the monastic day. It is an invitation to hear the sound of silence, to step out of clock time into the monastic flow of time, to stop, to reflect, to listen, to respond, and to come to a new understanding of the deep inner peace that silence and true listening can bring. As the liturgical book of hours is a series of psalms, hymns, reflections and prayers arranged to be chanted eight times a day, seven days a week on a four-week cycle, I designed this book in the same way, using short psalm extracts, reflections and prayers. I hope you will make this book your own and use it whatever way best helps you to build into your daily life moments of stillness and silence and to keep in touch with the rhythms and seasons of your heart.

You may of course use this book in any way that appeals to you. You may, for example, feel drawn to choose one hour that you will observe every day; or you might decide to choose two hours, one for the morning and the evening; or three, to give your day a beginning, middle and end using whatever hour is appropriate for the time you have chosen to mark these points in your day. Of course, if your daily routine allows it, you may find you can use most or even all of the hours each day, even if only for a short period.

Alternatively, you could choose an hour that suits

a particular time of the year – vespers in autumn, for example. Or you might find that a particular hour suits a particular season in your own life: thus for example you might choose matins at a time when you feel the need to trust the darkness in your life; or lauds at a time when you want to give thanks; or prime at a time when you need to be more reflective about what you do and how you do it; terce as a reminder of the importance of being in tune and connected with the rhythm of your life; sext at a time when you feel the need to renew your commitment and dedication; nones when you need to remind yourself of the impermanence and the endurance of all things; vespers when you want to feel reminded that you are not indispensable but part of the bigger picture; or you may choose compline at a time when you feel the need to surrender or to rest.

Another way you might use this book is to take a line or a stanza or a verse from any of the hours as a mantra for the day or for the week, so that you can have a chant in your heart every day. Or you may use a word or phrase from a psalm and link it with conscious breathing exercises. So for example, you might use your in-breath to become more conscious of your breathing, which helps you to become more centred; and as you breathe out you may use the word or phrase that appeals to you. Deliberate and conscious breathing in and out is the basis of meditation, and you can use a mantra or phrase from the psalms to give shape and meaning to this exercise.

Every day all over the world chants are sung by religious communities during what is known as the eight canonical hours. These hours are public services of praise and worship that take place at appointed times each day.

Some lay people also observe the hours, and one purpose of this book is to help people to do that in whatever way suits their lives.

The different hours mark the different 'seasons' of the day, and the pattern of the hours was designed to fit in with the natural rhythm of the day.

The eight hours are divided into three major choral offices and five 'little hours'. The eight hours are listed here, in order of occurrence, with the little hours indented:

- MATINS, takes place pre-dawn (also known as vigil or the nightwatch hour)

- LAUDS, happens at dawn, as darkness gives way to light

    - PRIME, takes place at morning, when work duties are given out in the monastery

    - TERCE, comes in the middle of the morning, at what is considered the third hour of the day

- SEXT, happens right in the middle of the day, at noon time, when people stop to eat

- NONES, is chanted as the day begins to decline in the mid to late afternoon

- VESPERS, occurs in the late afternoon, as evening falls

- COMPLINE, is the conclusion of the monastic day, as the community enters the night

This book is an attempt to preserve and hand on the spirit and values of a culture and a way of life that is rooted in the earth and touches the sky.

The special liturgical and monastic meaning of the word 'hour' goes back to the Greek word *hora*, which is older than our notion of a day consisting of twenty-four 60-minute periods, and the original religious notion of the hour is not so much a numerical measure of time but a soul measure.

The hours are the seasons of the day. Earlier generations, which were not ruled by alarm clocks or calendars, saw the hours as the way the day naturally ebbed and flowed through shades of light and darkness, as the day began, grew, blossomed, bore fruit and receded, with the same unfolding rhythm as everything that grows and changes on the earth.

Each hour has a character more complex than our sterile clock time. The hours provide a framework or a structure by which the monastic day is supported.

From the monastic perspective, time is a series of opportunities and encounters. When we live in the now we attune ourselves to the call of each moment, listening and responding to what each hour, each situation brings. This is very different from how most of us live our busy lives today, barely noticing the different qualities and characters of the stages of the day – pre-dawn, daybreak, early morning, late morning, high noon, afternoon, evening, nightfall. Saturated with information, our day is deprived of meaning and we are caught in a never-ending swirl of duties and demands, things to finish and things to put right.

This people's book of hours shows us that there is another way to live in this noisy, distracted world of ours and that this way is not as far out of our reach as we think. It speaks to our hearts because it is a universal call to enter the now, a call to stop, to listen, to hear the message of this moment.

It can speak to the contemplative in each of us. It speaks to our souls, which long for peace and connection to an ultimate source of meaning and value. It calls us to live in the present and puts us in touch with the rhythm of life, the rhythm of the universe. It helps us to become still, and reminds us to live lives that are directed by the spirit within us. It reminds us to live intentionally, not to be swept away by endless timetables, deadlines and agendas. It reminds us that though time is a precious commodity, it isn't as scarce as many of us believe. Above all, it teaches us that life is meant to be joyful. When we chant or recite the hours, we experience a deep joy that comes from within, from our own hearts.

Week 1

WEEK 1 | SUNDAY | PRIME

Your word is a lamp for my steps
and a light for my path.

– Psalm 119: 105

Listening to
divine whisperings
new life
new insights
a new reality

Listening to the stillness
before dawn breaks

Your will is my heritage,
forever the joy of my heart.

WEEK 1 | SUNDAY | LAUDS

My God You are my light and salvation.
Whom need I fear?

Psalm 27: 1

Dawn
 new life
 a genesis
 a new beginning
 a resurrection
 a promise
   as darkness moves
    into light

a time
 to give thanks
   for the gifts of life

The Lord is the strength of my life.

Week 1 | Sunday | Prime

For You alone are my hope Lord;
I have trusted You from my youth.

Psalm 71:5

Early Morning
  pregnant with
    hope
    goodness
    courage
      seeds of new beginnings

My life is an example to many, because You have been my strength and protection.

WEEK 1 | SUNDAY | TERCE

O praise the Lord, all you nations;
acclaim Him, all you peoples!
Strong is God's love for us;
the Lord is faithful forever.

Psalm 117: 1-2

Mid-morning
A time to
bless
  a word
  a smile
  a kindness
  a prayer
    in blessing
    my life is blessed

With humble heart I bless You, Lord.

Awakening Inner Peace

Week 1 | Sunday | Sext

Alleluia!
Open to me the gates of holiness:
I will enter and give thanks.
This is the Lord's own gate,
where the just may enter.
I will thank You for You have answered
and You are my saviour.

Psalm 118: 19–21

Midday –
    angelus bells
      an ancient Christian tradition
        calling us to pray
        to pray for peace.
– we pause to pray
    pray for peace

In You, O Lord, I have set my soul;
in silence and peace.

WEEK 1 | SUNDAY | NONES

How great is the goodness, Lord,
that You keep for those who fear You,
that You show to those who trust You
in the sight of all.

Psalm 31: 19

Aware of the
   impermanence
      transitoriness
         and limitations
            of this life
Aware of the
   permanence
   timelessness
   and mystery
      of eternal life

You, O Lord, are my rock, my stronghold.

WEEK 1 | SUNDAY | VESPERS

I will praise You, Lord my God, with all my heart
and glorify Your name forever,
for Your love to me has been great,
You have saved me from the depths of the grave.

Psalm 86: 12-13

Evening descends
light fades
day closes in
as silence falls
on the world

Setting aside our day
with serenity

The Lord gives grace and glory.

Week 1 | Sunday | Compline

If I should walk in the valley of darkness,
No evil would I fear.
You are there with your crook and your staff;
with these You give me comfort.

Psalm 23: 4

Receptivity
a condition of the night
entrusting the day with gratitude

Only goodness and faithful love will pursue me all
the days of my life.

WEEK 1 | MONDAY | MATINS

In the morning let me know Your love,
for I put my trust in You.
Make me know the way I should walk.

Psalm 143: 8

Waiting, listening
Opening to our inner selves
trusting each new moment
inviting us to hear
that small voice deep inside
the voice of God

To You I lift up my soul.

Week 1 | Monday | Lauds

Bless the Lord, O my soul;
all my being bless His holy name.

Psalm 103: 1

Early morning
rays of light come seeping in;
day breaks
   illuminating the sky
      a tapestry of reds, blues, yellows and golds
      an invitation to greet this new day
         with gratitude

Bless the Lord, O my soul, and never forget any of
His benefits.

WEEK 1 | MONDAY | PRIME

It is You, O Lord, who are my hope,
my trust, O Lord, since my youth.

Psalm 71: 5

Facing the unknown
    with hope
freeing us to
    go forth
        and embrace the goodness
        of this new day

My hope has always been in You.

WEEK 1 | MONDAY | TERCE

O Let the Earth bless the Lord,
to Him be highest glory and praise for ever.

Canticle of Daniel 3: 74

In Your likeness
    we are made
        in Your breath
          made divine

Embracing our
    humanity
      we are holy

To Him be highest glory and praise for ever.

WEEK 1 | MONDAY | SEXT

*Let everything that lives and that breathes give praise
to the Lord.*

Psalm 150: 6

Rhythmically
    pausing
        and breathing mindfully

Seeding our day
    With moments of stillness
        and peace

Praise God in His holy place.

WEEK 1 | MONDAY | NONES

Be a rock, a refuge for me,
a mighty stronghold to save me.

Psalm 31: 3

Resting in hope
aware of the hidden gifts
and graces available to us
Acknowledge the miracle of this day

For You are my rock, my stronghold.
For Your name's sake, lead me and guide me.

Awakening Inner Peace

Week 1 | Monday | Vespers

I will hear what the Lord has to say,
a voice that speaks of peace.

Psalm 85: 9

Resting in the peace of evening
  a time of reflection
  a time of healing
  a time of reconciliation

Moving forward in a spirit of quiet faith
    greeting in silence the descending darkness

Peace to those who turn to God.

WEEK 1 | MONDAY | COMPLINE

Surely goodness and kindness shall follow me
all the days of my life.

Psalm 23: 6

As night falls
   Being present each moment
      mindfully
      gracefully
  letting go of fear
  trusting the dark
    a time of serenity

In the Lord's own house shall I dwell
for ever and ever.

WEEK 1 | TUESDAY | MATINS

I am here and I call, You will hear me, O God.
Turn Your ear to me; hear my words.
Guard me as the apple of Your eye.

Psalm 17: 6,8

Setting aside time
  in the silence
    to be present
    to be attentive
    to be still
  peacefully entering
  and surrendering to the day

Hide me in the shadow of Your wings.

WEEK 1 | TUESDAY | LAUDS

In God is my safety and glory,
the rock of my strength.

Psalm 62: 8

Out of darkness
   the first flush of light
      new day
      new life
      new hope
      new strength

Take refuge in God, and trust Him at all times.

WEEK 1 | TUESDAY | PRIME

You are my God.
My happiness lies in You alone.

Psalm 16: 2

Prime
    A time for fortitude
      to face the day
    a time for resilience
        to begin again
          and again
A time of happiness
    a time for hope

Protect me God for I take refuge in You.

Week 1 | Tuesday | Terce

Make a joyful noise unto the Lord, all ye lands.
Serve the Lord with gladness: come before his presence with
singing.

Psalm 100: 1-2

Life
    God's life
        In us
        given
        blessed
            shared
            passed on
                through our humanity
                NOW

O All you works of the Lord, O Bless the Lord.
Be highest glory and praise for ever.

WEEK 1 | TUESDAY | SEXT

Bless the Lord of my soul;
let all my being bless Your holy name.

Psalm 103: 1

Believing we are protected
  we stop -
    to give thanks

Believing goodness awaits us
  we stop –
    to discover life's blessings
      we bless

Bless the Lord, my soul.

WEEK 1 | TUESDAY | NONES

Whoever dwells in the shelter of the most high,
will rest in the shadow of the Almighty.

Psalm 91: 1

Nones
  reminding us
    to do what we do
        well
        happily
        joyfully
        freely
  reminding us
    to live in the present moment
    in this wonderful moment

He is my refuge and my fortress, my God,
in whom I trust.

WEEK 1 | TUESDAY | VESPERS

Lord God, how great You are:
You made the moon to mark the months;
the sun knows the time for its setting.

Psalm 104: 19

In the cool of the evening
reflecting
on the gifts of the parting day.

We rest
and give thanks

Lord God, how great You are;
You are clothed with splendour and majesty.

Week 1 | Tuesday | Compline

Like the deer that yearns
for running streams,
so my soul is yearning
for You, my God.

Psalm 42: 2

In the quiet of the night
   Listening to
     the silence of the Earth
   Listening to the silence within

Moving
     into the centre of all silence
     where the spirit dwells

My soul is yearning for You, my God.

Week 1 | Wednesday | Matins

The Lord is my light and my help;
whom shall I fear?

Psalm 27: 1

Waiting in darkness
in silence
the gentle presence within
reminds us
this time is holy
this hour is holy
this moment is holy
we are holy

In the Lord I hold firm and take heart.

Week 1 | Wednesday | Lauds

In the morning You hear me;
in the morning I offer You my prayer,
watching and waiting.

Psalm 5: 4

A moment
waiting and watching
the sun filtering through
as day breaks

we give thanks
  a new day
  a new gift
  a new miracle

It is You whom I invoke, O Lord.

Week 1 | Wednesday | Prime

For Your love is better than life,
for my lips will speak Your praise.
So I will bless You all my life.

Psalm 63: 4-5

Consciously remembering
    who we are
    why we are here
    where we have come from
Remembering
    where we are going
    what we are drawn to
    why we do what we do

In Your name I will lift up my hands.

WEEK 1 | WEDNESDAY | TERCE

Let the Earth bless the Lord;
give Him glory and praise for ever.

Canticle of Daniel 3: 74

A time to give thanks for
the puff of air
the sound of bird song
the shadow across our path
the whispering of wind
the whiff of a rose
the glimmer of sunlight
A time to give thanks
for everything that lives and breathes

Night-time and day, O Bless the Lord.

WEEK 1 | WEDNESDAY | SEXT

It is God the Lord most high
Who gives each a place.

Psalm 87: 5, 7

Turning point
  in the day
time of
  renewal
  restoration
  Time to be still
Stillness
  Resting in our true home

In You all will find their home.

Week 1 | Wednesday | Nones

When I consider thy heavens, the work of thy fingers, the
moon and the stars, which thou hast ordained;
O Lord our Lord, how excellent is thy name in all the earth!

Psalm 8: 2

Nones
  time
to offer
            who we are
            what we have done
            what we have left undone
time
  to let go
    and relinquish
            possession of the day
  to give back freely
    what we have been freely given
  to give thanks

Ring out your joy to the Lord, O you just.

WEEK 1 | WEDNESDAY | VESPERS

God sends out word to the Earth,
and swiftly runs the command.
God showers down snow white as wool,
and scatters frost like ashes.

Psalm 147B: 15-16

Nature
  harmonious
  balanced
  ordered

Cycles of
    endings and beginnings
        sowing and reaping
        planting and harvesting
        spring and autumn
        morning and evening

O praise the Lord from the Heavens and the Earth.

WEEK 1 | WEDNESDAY | COMPLINE

O Lord, You have shown me my end,
how short is the length of my days.
Now I know how fleeting is my life.

Psalm 39: 5

Being fully present
gives new perspective
new significance to everything
deepening the sense of wonder
as day fades

In You rests all my hope.

WEEK 1 | THURSDAY | MATINS

O Lord, You search me and You know me,
You know my resting and my rising.

Psalm 139: 1-2

Before dawn
   reflecting on
      the
         mystery
            of life

coming to know
   that You, O God
      are always shaping us
         creating us
            in Your own likeness

All my ways lie open to You.

WEEK 1 | THURSDAY | LAUDS

Look towards God and be radiant;
let your faces not be abashed.

Psalm 34: 6

Dawn
greeting
welcoming
delighting in
this morning
as the first morning of creation

Taste and see that the Lord is good.
They are happy who seek refuge in God.

WEEK 1 | THURSDAY | PRIME

Make us know the shortness of our life,
that we may gain wisdom of heart.

Psalm 90: 12

Pausing
Breathing in God's presence
Pausing
Breathing out hopes for the day
Pausing
Breathing in Silence
Pausing
Breathing out acceptance of what is
Pausing
Breathing in stillness
Pausing
Breathing out peace

Lord, You have been our dwelling place.

WEEK 1 | THURSDAY | TERCE

I will bless the Lord at all times,
God's praise always on my lips.

Psalm 34: 2

Resting in
silence
and stillness
brings
comfort
support
inspiration
direction
courage
hope
peace
to this day

In the Lord my soul shall make its boast.
The humble shall hear and be glad.

WEEK 1 | THURSDAY | SEXT

A voice I did not know said to me,
"I freed your shoulder from the burden
your hands were freed from the load."

Psalm 81: 6-7

Late morning
enthusiasm flagging
reminding us to
stop
catch our breath
rest
reflect
make peace
find new joy
find new strength
in the moment

Sing aloud to God, our strength!

WEEK 1 | THURSDAY | NONES

Those who put their trust in the Lord
are like Mount Zion, that cannot be shaken,
that stands for ever.
On Israel, peace!

Psalm 125: 1, 5

Trusting in the Lord
we let go this day of
prejudice
negativity
hostility
reaching out with
tenderness
openness
gentleness
affirmation
and love

So the Lord surrounds His people.

Awakening Inner Peace

WEEK 1 | THURSDAY | VESPERS

Give thanks to the Lord, for he is good;
His love endures forever.

Psalm 118: 1

Each moment
an opportunity
to let go of the old
making space for the new
as we take leave of the day

Let us come before the Lord, giving thanks.

Week 1 | Thursday | Compline

You, O Lord, are my lamp,
my God who lightens my darkness.
With You I can break through any barrier.

Psalm 18: 29-30

Gratitude for the
gifts of the day
savouring
relishing
resting and
rejoicing
in what we have been given
Being blessed
we bless

With my God I can scale any wall.

WEEK 1 | FRIDAY | MATINS

When I see the Heavens, the work of Your hands,
the moon and the stars which You arranged;
how great is Your name, O Lord our God,
through all the Earth!

Psalm 8: 4, 10

You God of all the Earth
God of
Abraham and Sarah
Isaac and Rebecca
Jacob and Rachel.

beyond our understanding
unnamed,
eternal mystery

Who are we that You should keep us in mind,
mere mortals that You care for us?

WEEK 1 | FRIDAY | LAUDS

I will thank You, Lord, among the peoples,
among the nations I will praise You.
For Your love reaches to the Heavens,
and Your truth to the skies.

Psalm 108: 4-5

Waiting
watching
in the stillness
the world takes in a deep breath
birds awake
a crescendo of cacophonous twitters
salute the day
exhaling new life
echoing over the Earth
a time to give thanks

May Your glory shine on Earth!

WEEK 1 | FRIDAY | PRIME

In the morning, fill us with Your love;
we shall exult and rejoice all our days.
Give success to the work of our hands.

Psalm 90: 14, 17

Courage
  gift of the heart
    opening us to
        experience and
        accept ourselves
        as we are
        this day

Accepting ourselves
  awakens our love
  stirs our compassion
  melts our hardness
  frees our creativity
  opens our mind

Let the favour of the Lord be upon us.

Week 1 | Friday | Terce

Alleluia!
Give thanks to the Lord who is good,
for God's love endures forever.

Psalm 118: 1

Giving thanks
an invitation to stop
to listen
   to the quiet voice within
      the unheard voices around
      teaching us
      reminding us
         who it is
               we are
         where it is
               we are going
         reminding us
         that we are loved

The Lord's mercy endures forever.

Week 1 | Friday | Sext

God of hosts, bring us back;
Let Your face shine on us and we shall be saved.

Psalm 80: 4

Time to
sift
the gold from the dross
separate
what we need
and what we want
letting go
before we move
into the light

Give us life, and we will call upon Your name!

WEEK 1 | FRIDAY | NONES

What marvels the Lord worked for us!
Indeed we were glad.

Psalm 126: 3

Mid Day
   naming
   claiming
      our gifts
      our blessings
   giving thanks
      for what is good
      in ourselves
      in others
   sharing with gladness
      the marvels of our day
      the marvels of our God

The Lord has done great things for us.

WEEK 1 | FRIDAY | VESPERS

May God give you your heart's desire,
and fulfil every one of your plans.

Psalm 20: 4

Evening time
 a reminder
  that negativity
   is always
    lurking
    waiting
    to take hold
  negativity
   faced
   acknowledged
   confronted
   named
   claimed
    frees us
     to let it go
     to trust

May the Lord grant all your prayers.

WEEK 1 | FRIDAY | COMPLINE

In my anguish I called to You, Lord;
I cried to You, God, for help.

Psalm 118: 5

Returning home
  to ourselves
   drawing us
  into the mystery of night
    crying to God for help
   we gather our day
      offering it back to God
        in gratitude

From Your temple You heard my voice.

Week 1 | Saturday | Matins

To me, how mysterious Your thoughts,
the sum of them not to be numbered!
If I count them, they are more than the sand;
to finish, I must be eternal, like You.

Psalm 139: 17-18

Waiting
seeking You
God of our life
  seeking You with our mind
      You are beyond our grasp
  thinking we understand You
      You evade us
  seeking You in our heart
      You reveal yourself to us
        in our acceptance of the mystery

O search me, God, and know my heart.

Week 1: Saturday: Lauds

The Heavens proclaim the glory of God,
and the firmament shows forth the work of God's hands.
Day unto day takes up the story,
and night unto night makes known the message.

Psalm 19: 2-3

Creation
  beginning time
    before time
      in time
        all time
Creation
  ongoing story
      never complete
Creation
  arising out of emptiness
  returning to emptiness
      in a ceaseless rhythm
        of new beginnings
          from the hands of our creator

Your span extends to all the Earth.

WEEK 1 | SATURDAY | PRIME

Those who dwell in the shelter of the Most High,
and abide in the shade of the Almighty,
say to the Lord: "My refuge."

Psalm 91: 1-2

Pacing ourselves
   taking time to be still
   praying, meditating
   walking mindfully
      restoring our balance
      settling us down
our restless hearts
   finding refuge
      in the embrace of quiet
      in the silence of God

My stronghold, my God in whom I trust!

WEEK 1 | SATURDAY | TERCE

How lovely is Your dwelling place,
Lord, God of hosts.
My heart and my soul ring out their joy
to God, the living God.

Psalm 84: 2-3

Journeying inward
    discovering our heart's desire
        our true selves
           a place
                of joy
                of peace
                of hope
                of love
                Your dwelling place

My soul is longing and yearning,
is yearning for the courts of the Lord.

WEEK 1 | SATURDAY | SEXT

Remember Your word to Your servant,
by which You gave me hope.
This is my comfort in sorrow;
that Your promise gives me life.

Psalm 119: 49-50

Making space
    resting
        in the moment
    remembering
        the promise of life

Savouring
    this time
        with hope
        with wonder
    remembering
        to trust

Your Word is a lamp for my feet, a light on my path.

WEEK 1 | SATURDAY | NONES

I waited, I waited for the Lord,
Who stooped down to me,
and heard my cry.

Psalm 40: 1

Taking time
  to be
    to listen
      in silence
      drawn into inner wisdom
      and inner peace

**I waited patiently for the Lord; and He inclined
unto me, and heard my cry.**

WEEK 1 | SATURDAY | VESPERS

May God give you your heart's desire,
and fulfil every one of your plans.
May the Lord grant all your prayers.

Psalm 20: 5, 6

Abandoning ourselves
to the Lord
we pause
to give thanks
at even tide
relaxing in its fullness
as we freely let it go

May He answer us on the day that we call.

WEEK 1 | SATURDAY | COMPLINE

O come, bless the Lord,
all you who serve the Lord,
who stand in the house of the Lord,
in the courts of the house of our God.

Psalm 134: 1-2

Pondering
creation's story
recognising the universal rhythms
of day and night
sunsets and moon rises
of seas and seasons
stars surrendering to night
savouring its secrets

Bless the Lord through the night.

Week 2

O Lord, You search me and You know me,
You know my resting and my rising,
You discern my purpose from afar.

Psalm 139: 1

Creator God
　we can never comprehend You
　　Your beauty
　　　love
　　　goodness
　　　　are infinite
　　　　　beyond imagining

　Understanding You
　　You would not be infinite
　　You would not be God

All my ways lie open to You.

The God of gods, the Lord,
has spoken and summoned the Earth,
from the rising of the sun to its setting.
"Listen, my people, I will speak;
For I am God, your God."

Psalm 50: 1, 7

Listening to Silence
   we are still
The wise composer
  allows music
    to crescendo
     reach a climax
      and then –
        pause
        rest
        silence
        nothing
Listening to the sound in silence
  we hear the music

I am God your God.

The Lord is great and worthy of praise.
It was the Lord who made the Heavens;
His majesty and honour and power,
and splendour in the holy place.
Give the Lord the glory of His name.

Psalm 96: 4, 5-6, 8

God beyond time
    Timeless
    Eternal
    The ever-changing circle of time
        A reminder of eternity
    we think we have no time
    we are running out of time
Time is eternal -
    we have all the time
        we need
            always
    all time is ours
        NOW

Sing to the Lord a new song.

How lovely is Your dwelling place,
Lord God of Host.

Psalm 84: 1

Our world full of loveliness
    often hidden, tiny, fragile, abused
        needing to be
            supported
            protected
            acknowledged
            appreciated
            loved into being

Our world full of beauty, stopping
  we find it, finding
    we appreciate it, appreciating
      we embrace it, embracing
        we love it into being

If the Lord does not build the house,
in vain do its builders labour.

I have chosen the way of truth
with Your decrees before me.
I will run the way of Your commands;
You give freedom to my heart.

Psalm 119: 30, 32

Sabbath
  a space
  a time
    saying yes
      to the sacred

Sabbath
  a joy
  a freedom
    never a burden
    never a chore

Guide me in the way of Your commandments.

In the scroll of book it stands written
that I should do Your will.
My God I delight in Your law
in the depths of my heart.

Psalm 40: 8-9

Shadows lengthen
  day declines
    stopping
      we notice how our own will
        shaped our day

  we ask forgiveness
  we give thanks

I have never kept Your righteousness to myself.

Awakening Inner Peace

The Lord is King with majesty enthroned.
The world You have made firm not to be moved.
Your throne has stood firm from of old.
For all eternity O Lord You are.

Psalm 93: 1–2

No one lives by chance
   everyone, everything has a purpose
     a part to play
       in the grand design
         that is creation
           for all eternity

Every living breathing being
   is essential for Creation's completion
    - time to give thanks

Your decrees will never alter.

Why are you cast down, my soul?
Why groan within me?
Hope in God; I will praise yet again,
my saviour, my God.

Psalm 42: 6

Compline
   completing the circle of day
   mirroring the flow of life
      letting go with hope
         in trust

                  Time to give praise
                  Time to give thanks

When my soul is downcast within me,
I think of You.

My soul is waiting for the Lord.
I count on God's word.
My soul is longing for the Lord,
more than those who watch for daybreak.

Psalm 130: 5-6

Waiting
    in the dark
        trusting
        yearning
        longing
        believing
            God is coming
            as sure
            as light at daybreak

From the depths I call to You.

You crown the year with Your bounty,
abundance grows in Your path.
The meadows clothe themselves with flocks,
the valleys deck themselves with grain.
They shout and sing together with joy.

Psalm 65: 12, 14

Lauds
shout
sing
praise God
for the bounty
we have received
given freely
unconditionally
out of love
Time to stop
To reflect
on the rhythm
of this new day

Consider the lilies of the field;
they neither toil nor spin.

Open my eyes that I may see
the wonders of Your law.
I am a pilgrim on the Earth;
show me Your commands.

Psalm 119: 18–19

This day
    sets before us
        time to
            accept
            discover
            affirm
            delight
                in the
                    uniqueness
                    giftedness
                        that is ours
                            the unique beauty of all life

Your will is my delight, O God.

How many are Your works, O Lord!
In wisdom You have made them all.
The Earth is full of Your riches.

Psalm 104: 24

Terce
A time
to stop
to listen to ourselves
remembering
we carry everything we are
within us
A time to reflect
A time for gratitude
A time for wisdom

My God, how great You are!

Awakening Inner Peace

This is the work of the Lord,
a marvel in our eyes.
This day was made by the Lord;
we rejoice and are glad.

Psalm 118: 23-24

Sext
  noon- time
  lunch-time
  break-time
    restoring body
    replenishing energy
    resting soul
      a celebration
              alone
          with others
              rejoicing in the fruits of the Earth

Give thanks to the Lord for He is good.

Sing psalms to the Lord, you faithful ones,
give thanks to His holy name.
God's anger lasts a moment;
Gods favour all through life.

Psalm 30: 5-6

Afternoon
A time to reflect on all we have taken for granted
all we have regarded as our own
all we thought we achieved by ourselves

A time to give thanks
be mindful
alive to
all we have been given

In the evening, a spell of tears,
in the morning, shouts of joy.

I love You, Lord, my strength,
my rock, my fortress, my saviour.
God, You are the rock where I take refuge;
my shield, my mighty help, my stronghold.
Lord, You are worthy of all praise.
when I call I am saved from my foes.

Psalm 18: 1–4

Gratitude
    the key
        into full life
        into our true selves
Gratitude
    releases
        all fear and threat
    opens us to
        honesty
        integrity
        justice
        joy
        praise and happiness
Gratitude enriching our day

I take shelter in Him, my rock, my shield.

But You, Lord, are a shield about me.
I lie down to rest and I sleep.
I wake, for You uphold me.

Psalm 3: 4, 6

At Compline
  putting away the day
  preparing to rest
      aware of God's presence
      a time to rest
          as surely as
              a time to rise

When I am in trouble, You come to my relief.

Truly I have set my soul
in silence and peace,
like a weaned child on its mother's breast,
even so is my soul.
O Israel, hope in the Lord
both now and forever.

Psalm 131: 2-3

Waiting
in faith
with hope
in silence
finding
light in darkness
fullness in emptiness
peace in silence
contentment in God

I hope in the Lord both now and forever.

The Lord's is the Earth and its fullness,
the world and all its peoples.
It is God who set it on the seas;
who made it firm on the waters.

Psalm 24: 1-2

Dawn
  before the clatter of day
      in silence
      in solitude
          we hear a new day birthing
                  in us
                  around us
  out of silence
      the chant of lauds
              opens our heart
              quietens our mind
              restores our senses
                  as we enter the day
                  with new focus

The Lord's is the Earth and its fullness;
come, let us adore.

It was Your hands that made me and shaped me;
help me to learn your commands.
Your faithful will see me and rejoice,
for I trust in Your word.

Psalm 119: 73–74

A call to enter
into the mystery of who we are
  learning
    to trust
        uncertainty
        vulnerability
  discovering
    inner strength
    peace
    joy
        in the morning

Let Your love be ready to console me.

How many are Your works, O Lord!
In wisdom You have made them all.
The Earth is full of Your riches.

Psalm 104: 24

Terce
time to pause
bringing attention to our senses
source of
      undiluted pleasure
      joy unimagined
      never merited
      always available
        freely given to each of us
          out of love
            each day

I sing to the Lord all my life.

Bring an offering and enter God's courts,
worship the Lord in the temple.
O Earth, stand in fear of the Lord.

Psalm 96: 8-9

Taking time to
     stop
     bless
     eat
     nourish

Making space
     for ourselves
     for others
     for all creation

awareness
     at mid-day

Proclaim to the nations: "God is King."

Out of the depths I cry to You, O Lord,
Lord, hear my voice!
But with You is found forgiveness:
For this we revere You.

Psalm 130: 1–4

Forgiveness
the greatest of all giving

Forgiving
giving
to all who have
injured
hurt
abandoned
supported
helped us

**O let Your ears be attentive
to the voice of my pleading.**

How good and how pleasant it is,
when people live in unity!

Psalm 133: 1

Living in unity with all
part of the circle of life
continuously flowing
in the eternal interconnectedness of creation

For there the Lord gives blessing, life forever.

When You call I shall answer: "I am with you."
I will save you in distress and give you glory.

Psalm 91: 15

Compline
  allowing ourselves to be
                restored
                protected
                nourished
                supported
                sheltered
                    in the nest of the night

**With length of days I will content You; I shall let
You see my saving power.**

O God, save me by Your name,
by Your power, uphold my cause.
O God, hear my prayer,
listen to the words of my mouth.

Psalm 54: 1-2

Nelson Mandela
  27 years
    Imprisoned
    in darkness
    a source of light
Waiting with faith
  he became a light
    shining
      for his

          people
          party
          country
          world

I will sacrifice to You with willing heart.

- -

I lift up my eyes to the mountains;
from where shall come my help?
My help shall come from the Lord,
who made Heaven and Earth.

Psalm 121: 1–2

Stopping
silence
stillness
moving
into ourselves
listening to our inner voice
connecting with who we are
the emptiness of silence
becoming inexhaustibly full
of its fullness

He will keep your foot from stumbling,
your guard will never slumber.

To You have I lifted up my eyes,
You who dwell in the Heavens;
my eyes, like the eyes of slaves
on the hand of their lords.

Psalm 123: 1–2

Lifting up our voice
Lifting up our heart
letting go of falsehood
discovering
our true self
finding
love
joy
and freedom

So our eyes are on the Lord,
till He shows us His mercy.

Come, ring out our joy to the Lord;
hail the rock who saves us.
Let us come before God, giving thanks,
With songs let us hail the Lord.

Psalm 95: 1–2

Terce
Living the natural rhythm of day
  gives time to celebrate
      ourselves
      each other
      creation
      our creator
      time to give thanks

I called to the Lord in my distress;
He has answered and freed me.

O blessed are you who fear the Lord
And walk in God's ways!
By the labour of your hands you shall eat.
You will be happy and prosper.

Psalm 128: 1–2

Food
  - a form of meditation
Prepared with love
  appreciating
                smell
                taste
                colour
                presentation
      - a form of meditation
Received with love
  Remembering those who
        grew
        prepared
        cooked
        served
              - a form of meditation

He gives food to all living creatures,
for His mercy endures forever.

"I will not enter the house where I live nor go to the bed
where I rest.
I will give no sleep to my eyes,
To my eyelids I will give no slumber,
till I find a place for the Lord."

Psalm 132: 3–5

Afternoon
  lifting our hearts
    in gratitude
      for the gifts of the day
  God's forgiveness
    flowing through us into our world
      wiping out offence
bringing peace and joy

Let us go to the place of His dwelling;
let us bow down at His footstool.

Give thanks, and acclaim God's name,
make known God's deeds among the peoples.
O sing to the Lord, sing praise;
tell all His wonderful works!

Psalm 105: 1–2

Offering our day to God
less preoccupied
    with doing
    more aware of being
less preoccupied
    with the decisions
    more in tune with our deep desires
less attentive
    to reason and logic
    more attentive to our intuitions
less concerned
    with 'why'
    more open to
    discovering the resources within

Glory in His holy name;
let the hearts that seek the Lord rejoice.

Preserve me God, I take refuge in You.
I say to the Lord: "You are my God.
My happiness lies in you alone."

Psalm 16: 1–2

Giving ourselves over to sleep
    acknowledging
        our need for rest
    accepting
        our mortality
Letting go
    trusting only in God

I keep the Lord before me always.

The Lord is in His holy temple,
the Lord, whose throne is in Heaven,
whose eyes look down on the world.
The Lord is just and loves justice,
the upright shall see God's face.

Psalm 11: 4, 7

Darkness
predawn
trusting in God
with
faith
and love
new life
born within us
bringing
peace
courage
vision

The Lord is just and loves justice,
the upright shall see God's face.

The loving tenderness of our God,
who visits us from the dawn from on high;
He will give light to those in darkness,
those who dwell in the shadow of death,
and guide us into the way of peace.

The Canticle of Zacharias, Luke 1: 78-79

Dawn
 The tenderness of God
  cresting over the horizon
  consecrating the day
 - a morning offering
  consecrating us
   beginning our day
    anew
  Bringing peace

**He has looking favourably on His people and
redeemed them.**

O Lord, You search me and You know me,
O search me, God, and know my heart.
O test me and know my thoughts.
See that I follow not the wrong path,
and lead me in the path of life eternal.

Psalm 139: 1, 23–24

Accepting
our true self
unique
known and unconditionally loved
    filling us with
        gratitude
        joy
        peace

You Yourself know my resting and my rising;
You discern my thoughts from afar.

All the ends of the Earth have seen
the salvation of our God.
Shout to the Lord, all the Earth,
ring out your joy.

Psalm 98: 3–4

The more we bless
the more we are blessed!

Our blessings
never run out
drawn
from a bottomless source
replenished
eternally

O sing a new song to the Lord,
for He has worked wonders.

Your servant, Lord, Your servant am I;
You have loosened my bonds.
A thanksgiving sacrifice I make;
I will call on the Lord's name.

Psalm 116: 16–17

Sext
Giving thanks
connecting with our environment
reverencing the universe
co-creating the world today

How can I repay the Lord
for all His goodness to me?

For I know the Lord is great,
that our Lord is high above all gods.
Whatever the Lord wills the Lord does,
in Heaven, on Earth, in the seas.

Psalm 135: 5–6

Nones
   time of
         forgiveness
Forgiveness
   to fore give
         before
               during
                     after
                     any hurt or offence
Forgiveness
   a taste of divine grace
         pure gift

Praise the Lord, for the Lord is good.

Lord, what are we that You care for us,
mere mortals, that You keep us in mind,
creatures, who are merely a breath
whose life fades like a shadow?

Psalm 144: 3–4

Journeying towards the truth
   living with
      questions
      uncertainty
      ambiguity
   secure in not knowing
        answers becoming questions
        questions answers
          a gracefilled day
            lived to the full

He is my merciful love, my fortress;
He is my stronghold, my saviour.

To You, O Lord, I call,
my rock, hear me.
Hear the voice of my pleading,
as I call for help,
as I lift up my hands in prayer
to Your holy place.

Psalm 28: 1–2

Surrendering
  stepping out of the day
          into night
  setting aside our tasks
              a time to rest
Sleep
  a time of
          surrender
          grace
          sacredness
              a holy time

Hear the voice of my pleading
as I call for help.

O God, You are my God, for You I long,
for You my soul is thirsting.
My body pines for You,
like a dry, weary land without water.
So I gaze on You in the sanctuary,
to see Your strength and Your glory.

Psalm 63: 2-3

Gazing on God
in the sanctuary of our heart
darkness
invites us
to know
without knowing
in not knowing
we know

Your loving mercy is better than life;
my lips will speak Your praise.

Bless the Lord, my soul!
Lord God, how great You are,
clothed in majesty and glory,
wrapped in light as in a robe!

Psalm 104: 1–2

Blessing
Living
   now
      not in the past, in the dark
      not in the brightness of light
         yet to come
   only now
      in this moment
         experiencing
            consolation
            peace
            oneness
               the mystery of now
                  the mystery of God

How many are Your works, O Lord!
In wisdom You have made them all.

For Your love is better than life,
my lips will speak Your praise.
So I will bless You all my life,
in Your name I will lift up my hands.
My soul shall be filled as with a banquet,
my mouth shall praise You with joy.

Psalm 63: 4-6

The purpose of this day is to
  discover
  accept
        who we are
              unconditionally loved

The purpose of this day is to
  find the joy
        we were born to know,
              joy eternal

For You have been my strength;
in the shadow of Your wings I rejoice.

Sing psalms to the Lord with the harp,
with the sound of music.
With trumpets and the sound of the horn,
acclaim the King, the Lord.

Psalm 98: 5-6

Terce
aware of God's presence
doing what we do
> lovingly
> carefully
> attentively
> tenderly
> with gratitude
> with praise
> bringing inner peace
awareness of God
the message of terce

Let the rivers clap their hands,
and the hills ring out their joy.

Yes from this day forward,
all generations will call me blessed.
For the Almighty has done great things for me;
Holy is His name.

Canticle of Mary, Luke 1: 48-9

Sext
> a call to wholeness

Learning to
> trust ourselves
> follow our deepest desires
> explore the recesses of our heart
>> becoming whole

His mercy extends to those who fear Him,
from generation to generation.

Happy those whose offence is forgiven,
whose sin is remitted.
O happy those to whom the Lord
imputes no guilt,
in whose spirit is no guile.

Psalm 32: 1–2

Walking with our woundedness
accepting our brokenness
forgiving
ourselves and others
unconditionally
free
empowered
without guile
without blame
accepted unconditionally
the wisdom of maturity

To You I have acknowledged my sin;
my guilt I do not hide.

Rescue me, Lord, from my enemies;
I have fled to You for refuge.
Teach me to do Your will,
for You, O Lord, are my God.
Let Your good spirit guide me
in ways that are level and smooth.

Psalm 143: 9–10

Our spiritual journey
  the greatest human adventure –
      going beyond
          certainties
          doubts
      always journeying
          towards
          ever-unfolding truths

Make me know the way I should walk;
to You I lift up my soul.

Lord, who shall be admitted to Your tent
and dwell on Your holy mountain?
Those who walk without fault,
those who act with justice,
and speak the truth from their hearts.

Psalm 15: 1–2

The silence of the night
invites us to
detach ourselves from
possession of the day
entrusting it
entrusting ourselves
to the freedom of our God

Preserve me, O God,
for in You I take refuge.

Awakening Inner Peace

On my bed I remember You.
On You I muse through the night,
for You have been my help,
in the shadow of Your wings I rejoice.

Psalm 63: 7-8

Darkness
    our way
        into the gift
            of life

accepting the way of darkness
    we see light
    we know
            beyond logic
            beyond reason
                a way of love

My soul clings to You,
Your right hand holds me fast.

By God's word the Heavens were made,
by the breath of His mouth all the stars.
God collects the waves of the ocean,
and stores up the depths of the sea.

Psalm 33: 6–9

Dawn
   aware
      of the rhythm of giving and receiving
         in each day
            opening for us
               a new consciousness.
     Life anew
        new energy
   inviting us
      to give thanks

For God spoke; it came to be.

Not to us, Lord, not to us,
but to Your name give the glory,
for the sake of Your love and Your truth,
lest the heathen say: "Where is their God?"

Psalm 115: 1–2

In detachment
   we are free from small-mindedness
In awareness
   we take possession of ourselves
In letting go
   we live with ambiguity
In living with questions
   we wait for answers

Our God is in the Heavens;
He does whatever
He wills.

For You indeed are the Lord
most high above all the Earth,
exalted far above all spirits.
Rejoice, you just, in the Lord;
give glory to God's holy name.

Psalm 97: 9, 12

Terce
    stopping
        opening to the day
            blessing
            thanking
            appreciating life's gifts
    stopping
        celebrating life
    stopping
        being present to
            the source of life
            the immensity of life
            the infinity of love

Light shines forth for the just one,
and joy for the upright of heart.

O let the Earth bless the Lord,
to Him be highest glory and praise for ever.
And you mountains and hills, O bless the Lord.
And you, plants of the land, O bless the Lord.
And you fountains to springs, O bless the Lord.
To Him be highest glory and praise for ever.

Canticle of Daniel 3: 74–77

Wild flowers
  caressing the Earth with blessing

  pulling them up
          they bloom again
  paving the Earth
          they find a way through

  trampling them underfoot
          they blossom and bless

O give thanks to the Lord, because He is good;
because His mercy endures forever.

My song is of mercy and justice;
I sing to You, O Lord.
I will walk in the way of perfection.
O when, Lord, will You come?

Psalm 101: 1–2

Nones
stopping
  discovering
      recovering
          our true self
    exploring the
        breath
        height
        length
        depth
            of our inner being
        connecting with what lies beyond
                journey of the soul

I will walk with blameless heart
within my house.

For God has said only one thing;
only two do I know:
that to God alone belongs power,
and to You, Lord, love;
and that You repay us all,
according to our deeds.

Psalm 62: 12–13

Vespers
    evening drawing near
    darkness falling
            days work
                ending
                    letting go
                      ·offering it to God

In God alone be at rest, my soul,
for my hope is from Him.

And so my heart rejoices, my soul is glad;
even my body shall rest in safety.
For You will not leave my soul among the dead,
nor let Your beloved know decay.

Psalm 16: 9–10

Compline

Seeing with eyes of faith
trusting in the darkness
accepting with the simplicity of a child
surrendering to the protection of God
with thanksgiving

You will show me the path of life.

Week 3

I was thrust down, thrust down and falling,
but the Lord was my helper.
"The Lord's right hand has triumphed,
God's right hand raised me."

Psalm 118: 13–16

Without faith
darkness
frightening
disabling
With faith
light shines
through darkness
knowing light
we know
darkness itself is light

The Lord is my strength and my song.

The Heavens proclaim the glory of God,
and the firmament shows forth the work of God's hands.
There God has placed a tent for the sun;
it comes forth like a bridegroom coming from his tent,
rejoices like a champion to run its course.

Psalm 19: 2, 6

Each new day
  gifting us with new freedom
      to proclaim the glory of God
    a tent of freedom
      to start anew
          out of love not necessity
    a divine freedom
        empowering us
        graciously inviting
        never forcing
        respectfully calling us to human freedom

The law of the Lord is perfect;
it revives the soul.

If you trust in the Lord and do good,
then you will live in the land and be secure.
If you find your delight in the Lord,
He will grant your heart's desire.

Psalm 37: 3–4

Waiting
in faith
in silence
we learn to
believe in ourselves
in others
transforming problems into possibilities

Be still before the Lord
and wait in patience.

Let the Heavens rejoice and Earth be glad;
let the sea and all within it thunder praise.
Let the land and all it bears rejoice.

Psalm 96: 11–12

Looking at a flower
  knowing the flower
  being the flower
      becoming its root, stem, bud
Noticing the dew
being the dew
      glistening in the silence
      breathing freshness
      nestling between blossoms
Becoming ourselves
  here, now, today
    growing, blossoming,
    blooming, blessing, radiating
      peacefully, happily, joyfully, contentedly
        accepting who we are not who we want to be

**Tell among all the nations His glory, and His
wonders among all the peoples.**

Remember Your word to your servant,
by which you gave me hope.
This is my comfort in sorrow;
that Your promise gives me life.
Though the proud may utterly deride me,
I keep to Your law.

Psalm 119: 49–51

Sabbath
    rest
    restoration
    refreshment
    breathing in
    and breathing out
        thanksgiving, peace, joy
Sabbath
      remembering with
        tenderness, love, wonder, joy
            the beauty of our world
            the beauty of our day

In Your commands I have found my delight.

I will greatly bless her produce,
I will fill her poor with bread.
I will clothe her priests with salvation,
and her faithful shall ring out their joy.

Psalm 132: 15–16

Nones
  stepping back
  harvesting
        the gifts of the day
              giving thanks
                    holding not grasping
tasting with sweetness
        peace
        serenity
        wellbeing
        delight

This is my resting-place forever,
here I have chosen to live.

Rescue me from those who pursue me
For they are stronger than I.
Bring my soul out of this prison,
and then I shall praise Your name.
Around me the just will assemble,
because of Your goodness to me.

Psalm 142: 7–8

Vespers
  stopping, reflecting
  Listening to
      the small voice within, confronting our own fears
      reducing the power of darkness
              making the hostile hospitable
              the strange familiar
              finding new meaning
                  we affirm life

Listen, then, to my cry,
for I am in the depths of distress.

But I through the greatness of Your love,
have access to Your house.
I bow down before Your holy temple,
filled with awe.

Psalm 5: 8

Night-time
    Reflecting on our day
            being grateful
            fore-giving
            confronting our fears with faith
            looking back
            leaning forward

Lead me, Lord, in Your justice.

I called to the Lord in my distress;
God answered and freed me.
The Lord is at my side; I do not fear.
What can mortals do against me?
The Lord is at my side as my helper;
I shall look down on my foes.

Psalm 118: 5-7

Matins
  reminding us
    to trust the night
        its fearsomeness
        its awesomeness
              only through darkness
              we know light

The Lord is my strength and my song.

The law of the Lord is perfect,
it revives the soul.
The rule of the Lord is to be trusted,
it gives wisdom to the simple.
The precepts of the Lord are right,
they gladden the heart.

Psalm 19: 8–9

In the silence and stillness of dawn
emptying ourselves of trivia
tuning
into our inner self
tuning into
God's call in us
reminding us
who we are
where we are going
how we journey this day

Your decrees, O Lord,
are just and all of them true.

You stretch Your hand and save me,
Your hand will do all things for me.
Your love, O Lord, is eternal,
Discard not the work of Your hands.

Psalm 138: 7–8

Living with

    polarities

    paradoxes

    contradictions

        the secret of inner happiness

Accepting without understanding

    honouring difference

        finding unity in diversity

            we move joyfully into the day

The Lord is high yet looks on the lowly,
and the haughty, God knows from afar.

I will praise You, Lord, with all my heart;
I will recount all Your wonders.
I will rejoice You and be glad,
and sing psalms to Your name, O Most High.

Psalm 9: 2-3

Living by
>> achievements
>> attainments
>> ambitions
>> goals
>> expectations
we forget to wonder

Terce
>> a time to wonder
>> and be glad

You will not forsake those who seek You, O Lord.

Happy are those who fear the Lord,
who takes delight in all God's commands.
Their descendants shall be powerful on the Earth;
the children of the upright are blessed.

Psalm 112: 1-2

Sext
    a time
        to reflect on
            enough
        to remember
            that *enough* is *enough*
recognise
    enough
a time
to know
    when *enough* is *enough*

A time of gratitude

A light rises in the darkness for the upright.

Those who are sowing in tears,
will sing when they reap.
They go out, they go out, full tears,
carrying seed for the sowing;
they come back, they come back, full of song,
carrying their sheaves.

Psalm 126: 5-6

Nones
  stopping to pray
      surrendering our desires
      relishing our gifts
      giving thanks
          knowing
                peace
                joy
                gratitude
                love
                freedom

Deliver us, O Lord, from our bondage.

But as for me, I trust in You, Lord;
I say: "You are my God.
My life is in Your hands, deliver me
from the hands of those who hate me.
Let Your face shine on Your servant.
Save me in Your love."

Psalm 31: 15–17

In the peace of the evening
    gathering together
        our day
accepting it for what it is
        in all its light and shadow
the gift of evening

Be strong, let your heart take courage,
all who hope in the Lord.

How many, O Lord my God,
are the wonders and designs
that You have worked for us;
You have no equal.
Should I proclaim and speak of them,
they are more than I can tell!

Psalm 40: 6

In the sacredness of the night
we move beyond the visible
into the core of our being
where we know we are
known completely
loved unconditionally
by our creator

Blessed the man who has placed
his trust in the Lord.

Awakening Inner Peace

I have called to You, Lord, hasten to help me!
Hear my voice when I cry to You.
Let my prayer rise before You like incense,
the raising of my hands like an evening oblation.

Psalm 141: 1-2

The silence of darkness
    listening
        to our inner voice
    hearing
        in the depth of our heart
understanding
        what we are being called to
        what is being asked of us
          at this time
            in this place

To You Lord God, my eyes are turned,
in You I take refuge, spare my soul!

Cry out with joy to God all the Earth,
O sing to the glory of His name,
rendering glorious praise.
Say to God: "How tremendous Your deeds!
Come and see the works of God,
tremendous deeds for the people."

Psalm 66: 1–3, 5

Unaware	Dawn
	repetitious
	inevitable
	taken for granted
	ingratitude
Aware	Surprised by sunrise
	it flows through our senses
	transforming us with lithesomeness
	gracefulness
	gratefulness.

Surprised by sunrise
  we take nothing for granted
  we see and experience
    God's miracles everywhere

O peoples, bless our God;
let the voice of His praise resound.

I thank You, Lord, with all my heart,
You have heard the words of my mouth.
In the presence of the angels I will bless You.
I will adore before your holy temple.

Psalm 138: 1–2

God in   everyday, everything, everyone
God in   clouds and sky
          sun and moon
          trees and flowers
          creatures of sky and sea
          lakes and rivers
          mountains and hills
          showers and rain
          tears and laughter
          night and day
          darkness and light
          breezes and wind
          fire and water
          air and Earth.
God in everything
God in everyone
God closer to us than ourselves

O Lord, Your merciful love is eternal.

So I gaze on You in the sanctuary
to see Your strength and Your glory,
for Your love is better than life,
my lips will speak Your praise.

Psalm 63: 3–4

Living with affluence
wanting more
enlarged vessels
rarely full
never over-flowing
never satisfied

Staying close
to the source of life
needs diminish
vessels reduce
always full
over-flowing
with joy
with gratitude

My soul clings fast to You;
Your right hand upholds me.

Good people take pity and lend,
they conduct their affairs with honour.
The just will never waver,
they will be remembered for ever.
Openhanded, they give to the poor;
their justice stands firm for ever.
Their heads will be raised in glory.

Psalm 112: 5-6, 9

Sext   a time to listen
to the signs of our time

a time to listen
to the cry of the poor

a time to reflect
with openhandedness
openheartedness

a time to give thanks
for all that is given to us

With firm hearts we trust in the Lord.

I will give You glory, O God my king,
I will bless your name for ever.
You are just in all Your ways,
and loving in all Your deeds.
You are close to all who call You,
who call on You from their hearts.

Psalm 145: 1, 17-18

Nones-time
    withdrawing
        with gratitude
        recognising enough
        counting our blessings
        giving thanks for everything.

Let my mouth speak the praise of the Lord.

Awakening Inner Peace

The eyes of the Lord are toward the just,
and His ears toward their appeal.
The Lord ransoms the souls of the faithful.
None who trust in God shall be condemned.

Psalm 34: 16, 23

Reflecting on our day
we find what is sacred

Through our senses
the spirit speaks

Walking our path of life
we tread on holy ground

Ordinary every day events and things
radiate the divine

All who trust in Him shall not be condemned.

You are kind and full of compassion,
slow to anger, abounding in love.
How good You are, Lord to all,
compassionate to all your creatures.

Psalm 145: 8–9

Looking deeply within
knowing we are loved unconditionally
releasing us from fear
healing us from our wounds
freeing us to be ourselves
bringing peace
at night

All Your creatures shall thank You, O Lord,
and Your friends shall repeat their blessing.

Have mercy on me, God have mercy,
for in You my soul has taken refuge.
In the shadow of Your wings I take refuge,
till the storms of destruction pass by.

Psalm 57: 2

God

  always waiting to enlighten

    all night long

      Jacob struggled

        with the angel of darkness

  at dawn

      struggle finished

        Jacob's angel blessed him

          with a disability

  pre dawn

      we too struggle with the angel of darkness

  at dawn

      accepting our shadow and light

        we are blessed knowing

          our weakness is our strength

**I call to You God the most high, to You who have
always been my help.**

Give thanks to Lord upon the harp,
with a ten-stringed lute play your songs
Sing to the Lord a song that is new,
play loudly, with all your skill.

Psalm 33: 1–3

Being grateful
an outward thrust
we become
less concerned
with what is missing
more focused
on sharing
what is given
this day

I will ring out with joy to You, O my God.

Your will is wonderful indeed;
therefore I obey it.
Turn and show me Your mercy;
show justice to Your friends.
Let my steps be guided by Your promise.

Psalm 119: 129–133

Living intentionally
    demands discipline
    heightens our consciousness
    develops our sensitivity.

As musicians, athletes, dancers
    benefit from the discipline of routine
        we unfold with
            vitality
            joy
            sensitivity
              from a daily spiritual routine

**I am Your servant; give me understanding: then I
shall know Your decrees.**

Blessed are those whom You choose and call
to dwell in your courts.
We are filled with the blessings of Your house,
of Your holy temple.

Psalm 65: 5

Terce
a time
to recognise our gifts
realise our potential
live our dream
The best we can be this day
is already within

You are the hope of all the Earth,
and of far distant isles.

Lord, let Your love come upon me,
the saving help of Your promise.
I shall keep Your law always,
for ever and ever.

Psalm 119: 41, 44

Sext
  a call
      to simplicity

Simplicity
  living close to the limits of our resources
      with spontaneity and truthfulness

Simplicity
      achieved through
          conscious, consistent
          reflection and discernment
              in honesty
              with generosity by grace

Lord, I trust in Your word.

Let me dwell in Your tent for ever,
and hide in the shelter of Your wings.
For You, O God, hear my prayer;
grant me the heritage of those who fear You.

Psalm 61: 5–6

Suffering humanity
  accepting
      our finite selves
         in the face of infinity
  experiencing blessings
    in suffering
    in all things

From the end of the Earth I call;
my heart is faint.

Yes, it was You who took me from the womb,
entrusted me to my mother's breast.
To You I was committed from my birth,
from my mother's womb You have been my God.
Do not leave me alone in my distress;
come close, there is none else to help.

Psalm 22: 10–12

One journey
  two paths
     the outer path
        career, work, busyness
     the inner path
        heart space hidden.

An integrated day
    travelling both paths
at one time
    in Gods time

Stay not far from me; trouble is near,
and there is no one to help.

Look at me, answer me, Lord my God!
Give light to my eyes lest I fall asleep in death.
As for me, I trust in Your merciful love.
Let my heart rejoice in Your saving help.

Psalm 13: 4, 7

Our shadow
  follows us
    everywhere
    every day
        unrecognised
          disowned
          cast aside
              it frightens
              confronts
              challenges us
        recognised
        claimed
        named
          it illuminates
          guides
          comforts
          brings peace
              at night

Let me sing to You Lord for Your goodness to me

My heart is ready, O God,
my heart is ready.
I will sing, I will sing Your praise.
Awake, my soul,
awake, lyre and harp,
I will awake the dawn.

Psalm 57: 8-9

Matins

calling us to wakefulness
a kind word
thought
disappointment
loss
mistake
new dream
vision
everything
calling us to see and hear
with open hearts

O God, arise above the Heavens, may Your glory shine on Earth!

Alleluia!
Sing a new song to the Lord,
sing praise in the assembly of the faithful.
Let Israel rejoice in its Maker;
let Zion's people exult in their king.

Psalm 149: 1-6

Recalling
    the abundance of gifts given to us
        unmerited
        gratuitously
            we are moved to give thanks at morning.
Gratitude in itself brings happiness
In time learning
    to give thanks for everything
        loss and gain
        conflict and peace
        sorrow and joy
        sickness and health.
Gratitude always brings happiness

May the praise of God be on my lips.

Examine me, Lord, and try me;
O test my heart and my mind,
for Your love is before my eyes
and I walk according to Your truth.

Psalm 26: 2–3

The way of truth
> tests our heart
> examines our motivation
> relieves our suffering
> challenges our commitment
> lies in loving perseverance
> and always bears fruit

O Lord, I love the house where You dwell, the place where Your glory abides.

Do not be afraid for I have redeemed you,
I have called you by your name, you are mine.
Should you pass through the seas, I will be with you,
or through rivers, they will not swallow you up.
Should you walk through fire you will not be scorched
and the flames will not burn you.
For I am Yahweh, your God, the holy one of Israel,
your saviour.

Isaiah 43 : 1–3

Terce
Calling to
> serenity
> tenderness
> honesty
> trust
> compassion
Calling to
> accept ourselves unconditionally
> > every day

Do not be afraid, for I am with you.

I shall walk in the path of freedom,
for I seek Your precepts.
I will speak of Your will before the powerful
and not be abashed.

Psalm 119: 45–46

Wholeness
  balancing being and doing
          the call of mid-day
          the call of sext
Doing
  moving
          with focused attention
          accomplishing specific tasks
          achieving goals
Being
  pondering
  centred
  fully present
  each moment
  with receptive awareness
  to God's call

**I will worship Your commands and love them, and
ponder Your statutes.**

"What can bring us happiness?" many say.
Lift up the light of Your face on us, O Lord.
You have put into my heart a greater joy
than they have from abundance of corn and new wine.

Psalm 4: 7–8

Loneliness
    a universal human condition
Loneliness
    rejected
    denied
    avoided
        brings
            alienation
            isolation
Loneliness
    faced
    discerned
    understood
    accepted
        brings
            health
            happiness
            peace

I will lie down in peace and sleep comes at once,
for You alone, Lord, make me dwell in safety.

Praise the Lord from the Earth,
sea creatures and all oceans,
all mountains and hills,
all fruit trees and cedars,
beasts, wild and tame,
reptiles and birds on the wing.

Psalm 148: 7–10

Daylight fading
   reflected
in shadows
      changing shape and form
flowers
plants
      prepare themselves for night
         an enclave of nature
            at the heart of the Earth
monks and nuns
         offering
            vespers
            in cloister
               an enclave of love
               at the heart of the universe

Praise the Lord from the Earth.

Lord, hear a cause that is just;
pay heed to my cry.
Turn Your ear to my prayer,
no deceit is on my lips.
You search my heart, You visit me by night.
You test me and You find in me no wrong.
There was no faltering in my steps.

Psalm 17: 1, 3, 5

The shadow self
    belongs to the self
    controls the self
        as long as the self
            rejects
            represses it
The shadow self
    accepted
    confronted
    loved
    forgiven
        frees us into our true selves
          to rest in peace

Turn your ear to me; hear my words.

In God alone be at rest, my soul
from God comes my hope.
God alone is my rock, my stronghold
my fortress, I stand firm.

Psalm 62: 2-3

Rejecting
  our aloneness
  our emptiness
    living
      according to the expectations of others
                always looking for someone
                  something
                  anything
                  to fill our inner emptiness
Accepting our emptiness
  embracing our aloneness
    we grow and blossom
      finding
        the person we are called to be our true selves

Pour out our hearts to the Lord,
for God is our refuge.

God be merciful unto us, and bless us;
and cause his face to shine upon us;
That thy way may be known upon earth,
thy saving health among all nations.

Psalm 67: 2-3

Today
With gratitude and praise
    we make peace with our world
        with everything in our life
            acknowledging everything
            light and shadow
            as part of us
            we become whole

To Him be highest glory and praise forever.

I have sought You with all my heart;
let me not stray from Your commands.
I treasure Your promise in my heart,
I rejoiced to do Your will.
I take delight in Your statutes;
I will not forget Your word.

Psalm 119: 10-11, 16

God beyond all understanding
bringing balance and harmony
to the
boundless resources
powerful energies
store of strength
endless potential
of our being

Open my eyes, that I may see
the wonder of Your law.

I give Egypt for your ransom
and exchange Cush and Sheba for you,
because you are precious in my eyes,
because you are honoured and I love you.

Isaiah 43: 3-4

Living from our heart
a deeper way of knowing
Living from our heart
praising
with thanksgiving
with love
Living from our heart
giving
forgiving
healing

Living from our heart
wholeness
forgiveness
celebration

Do not be afraid, for I am with you.

Bend my heart to Your will,
and not to selfish gain.
Keep my eyes from what is false;
by Your word, give me life.
See, I long for Your precepts;
then in Your justice, give me life.

Psalm 119 : 36–37, 40

Sext
  calling us
      to the simplicity
          of a child
      to live life in the moment
              listening to our inner voice
              connecting with our spirit
                  without distortion
                  or destruction

Lord, let Your mercy come upon me.

Blessed be the Lord who has shown me
such a steadfast love in a fortified city.
Be strong, let your heart take courage,
all who hope in the Lord.

Psalm 31: 22, 25

Nones
   twilight time
   time between two worlds
Nones
     frenzied world quietens
           light recedes
           darkness deepens
                 the unhurried pace
                     of the new world takes over
       our world united
           in formlessness
                 the twilight of day
                 the twilight of life

The Lord guards the faithful.

Let us praise the name of the Lord,
who alone is exalted.
The splendour of God's name
reaches beyond Heaven and Earth.

Psalm 148: 13

Time in the evening
connected with the Earth
roots us in reality
relieves us from
anxieties
self-centredness
self-importance
seeing ourselves as part of creation
Time in the evening
connected with ourselves
with all creation
in touch with the
splendour of our being
splendour of the universe
a transforming experience

He is the praise of all His faithful.

My soul shall live for God and my children too shall serve.
They shall tell of the Lord to generations yet to come;
declare to those unborn, the faithfulness of God.
"These things the Lord has done."

Psalm 22: 31–32

Compline
    a time to
        forgive
        radiate goodness
        acknowledge the sacred
        bless creation
        call forth the best
            that is in all things

All the Earth shall remember
and return to the Lord.

When You went forth, O God, at the head of Your people,
when You marched across the desert, the Earth trembled,
the Heavens melted at the presence of God,
at the presence of God, Israel's God.

Psalm 68: 8-9

Walking the road of life
  we are called
      to journey
         into ourselves
            into the vast interior of our psyche
              of our soul
              of our heart.
Called from
     safety
     comfort
     knowing
        into the unknown
        challenged
        to stay on the road
        to trust our inner wisdom

God gives the desolate a home to dwell in.

- -

Cry out with joy to the Lord, all the Earth.
Serve the Lord with gladness.
Come before Him singing for joy.

Psalm 100: 1–2

God's joy
Always in us
  given to us out of love
  each day
  each moment
    fully
    always
Joy
  cannot be organised
  cannot be planned
    need only
      be desired
        it finds us
In transcending what we
  think we can do
  think we can be
    joy always surprises

Serve the Lord with gladness.

The Lord is your guard and your shade,
and stands at your right.
By day the sun shall not smite you,
nor the moon in the night.

Psalm 121: 5–6

Presence
    sacred experience
        in stillness
    healing experience
        in pain
    graced experience
        in oneness
    joyful experience
        in celebration
            always there for us

O Lord, be my guard and my shade.

The Lord will guard you from evil,
He will guard your soul.
The Lord will guard your going and coming,
both now and for ever.

Psalm 121: 7–8

Earth
    strong, steady, serene, supportive
Air
    light and free, formless
Fire
    heat, bright, energetic
Water
    flowing, swerving
Earth, air, fire and water
    in us, around us, part of us, protecting us
    connecting us with
            ourselves
            each other
            the universe
            our God

My help shall come from the Lord.

You are my shelter, my shield;
I hope in Your word.
Let my hopes not be in vain.

Psalm 119: 114, 16

Aware or unaware
  we create our own solutions
    our own reality
      by choice or by chance

Aware
  now
    we choose
      our own reality
      the desires of our heart
    we choose
      inner peace with joy and hope

I will keep my God's commands.

The mouths of the just speak wisdom,
and their lips say what is right;
the love of their God is their heart,
their steps shall be saved from stumbling.

Psalm 37: 30-1

Living in falsehood
    disconnected from truth
    alienated from reality

Living in truth
    healed
    empowered
    moving beyond alienation
    anchored in reality
    experiencing inner peace
        we move through the day

Mark the blameless, observe the upright; for the peaceful man a future lies in store.

Alleluia!
O give thanks to the Lord who is good,
whose love endures for ever.
Give thanks to the God of gods,
whose love endures for ever.
Give thanks to the Lord of lords,
whose love endures for ever.

Psalm 136: 1–3

Evening
   Listening with our heart
      we come to know the
            shape
            colour
            smell
            touch
            sound
               of the day
                     and its message for us
            Giving thanks

To the God of Heaven give thanks,
for His mercy endures forever.

O Lord, plead my cause against my foes;
fight those who fight me.
Take up Your buckler and shield;
arise to help me.
O Lord, say to my soul:
"I am your salvation."

Psalm 35: 1–3

To move beyond our fears
  we must move into them
      acknowledging
      naming
      owning
      accepting them
            accepting ourselves unconditionally
            our fears
                  dissipate
                  disappear
                        lose their power over us

Vindicate me, Lord, my God,
in accord with Your justice.

Week 4

For God has said only one thing,
only two do I know,
that to God alone belongs power
and to You, Lord, love,
and that You repay us all
according to our deeds.

Psalm 62: 12- 13

Matins
   the call
      to journey into ourselves
         to find our unknown-ness within

      journeying into ourselves

         we let go of falsity
           to discover truth
           the true self

In God alone be at rest, my soul,
for my hope is from Him.

Alleluia!
Praise the Lord from the Heavens,
Praise God in the heights.
Praise God, all you angels,
Praise Him, all you host.
Praise God, sun and moon,
Praise Him, shining stars.
Praise God, highest Heavens
And the waters above the Heavens.

Psalm 148: 1–4

Lauds
A time of joy and praise

Joy and praise
    is ours
        when we do
           what we do
               in freedom and integrity of heart

Let us praise the name of the Lord.

When I see the Heavens, the work of Your hands,
the moon and the stars which You arranged,
what are we that You should keep us in mind,
mere mortals that You care for us?

Psalm 8: 4-5

Miracle of humanity
    stemming from
        'humus', the Earth
    remembering
        we are of the Earth
Breath of God
    enfolding us
    consecrating us
    blessing us
    reminding us
        we are human and divine

How great is Your name, O Lord our God,
through all the Earth.

Lord, I long for Your saving help,
and Your law is my delight.
Give life to my soul that I may praise You.
Let Your decrees give me help.

Psalm 119: 174–5

Balancing
  being and doing
  life and work
        brings harmony and contentment
                to every experience
        encourages us to
                come alive to our true selves
        fills us
                with the life of the spirit
      opens us to
                receive what life is offering us NOW

My tongue will sing of Your promise,
for Your commands are just.

O send forth Your light and Your truth;
let these be my guide
Let them bring me to Your holy mountain,
to the place where You dwell.

Psalm 43: 3

Sext

    a time to stop

        reflect

        accept what has been

        live in the present

    a time to

        pause

        commit to the future

            with

                confidence

                strength

                courage

I will praise Him yet again,
my saving presence and my God.

O Lord, I cried to You for help,
and You, my God, have healed me.
O Lord, You have raised my soul from the dead,
restored me to life from those who sink into the grave.

Psalm 30: 3–4

Nones
  aware of our fraility
  recognising our brokenness
  connecting with the frailty of all humanity
Nones
  accepting
    all that divides
    all that unifies
    all that is broken
      knowing peace

I will praise You, Lord, for You have rescued me.

It was God who made the great lights,
whose love endures for ever.
The sun to rule in the day,
whose love endures for ever.
The moon and stars in the night,
whose love endures for ever.

Psalm 136: 7–9

At the core of our being
   we are all one
      in the unity of all things
   drawn together
      as we affect
         and are affected by each other
   a centre of gravity
      in the heart of creation

O give thanks to the Lord, for He is good.

O Lord, listen to my prayer
and let my cry for help reach You.
Do not hide Your face from me
in the day of my distress.
Turn Your ear towards me,
and answer me quickly when I call.

Psalm 102: 2–3

Night
  A time to
      surrender
      rest
      wait
      yield
        to the transforming power of sleep

You, O Lord, are enthroned forever.

O Lord, You have been my refuge
from one generation to the next.
Before the mountains were born
or the Earth or the world brought forth,
You are God, without beginning or end.

Psalm 90: 1-2

The journey into God
    never complete
a journey of
    uncovering
    reclaiming
    gathering
    integrating
    discovering what is lost
a journey of light and darkness

You sweep us away like a dream,
like grass which springs up in the morning.

O sing a new song to the Lord,
sing to the Lord all the Earth.
O sing to the Lord, bless His name.
Proclaim God's help day by day.
Tell among the nations His glory,
and His wonders among all the peoples.

Psalm 96: 1–3

Dawn
  a special moment of wonder
    a new moment
        unmerited

Lauds
  reminding us to
        awaken to the wonders of dawn
        open to the unexpected
        rejoice in each moment

The Lord is great and highly to be praised.

You founded the Earth on its base,
to stand firm from age to age.
You wrapped it with the ocean like a cloak;
the waters stood higher than the mountains.

Psalm 104: 5–6

Knowing
>the happiness of
>>an integrated life
>>>we bring body, mind and spirit into
>>>>what we do
>>>>who we are
>>>living and loving one continuum -
>>>>satisfying our deepest yearnings

Bless the Lord my soul; let all my being
bless Your holy name.

Lord how I love Your law!
It is ever in my mind.
Your command makes me wiser than my foes,
for it is mine for ever.
I have more insight than all who teach me
for I ponder Your will.
I have more understanding than the old,
for I keep Your precepts.

Psalm 119: 97–100

Awareness
    giving perspective
        to the journey of life

Journeying
    with awareness
    with attention
    with mindfulness
        each event unique
        each step
            a new beginning

Your word is a lamp for my feet,
and a light for my path.

Let this be written for ages to come
that a people yet unborn may praise the Lord;
for the Lord leaned down from the sanctuary on high,
and looked down from Heaven to the Earth,
in order to hear the groans of the prisoners,
and free those condemned to die.

Psalm 102: 19–21

A piece of bread
slice of fruit
cup of tea
  become
      a sacred meal
           when taken quietly mindfully
              in awareness alone with
others
      a moment of togetherness
      of sharing
      of thanks
      a celebration
      a prayer of praise

**He will turn to the prayers of the helpless; He will
not despise their prayers.**

....

The Lord listened and had pity.
The Lord came to my help.
For me You have changed my mourning into dancing,
You removed my sackcloth and clothed me with joy.
So my soul sings psalms to You unceasingly.
O Lord my God, I will thank You for ever.

Psalm 30: 11–13

Nones
    Accepting ourselves
    accepting others
allowing
    our weaknesses
    others' weaknesses
        transform us
opening
to the new moment
    with new awareness
      new heart

To You, Lord, I cried, to my God I made appeal.

My soul, give thanks to the Lord,
all my being, bless God's holy name.
My soul, give thanks to the Lord
and never forget all God's blessings.

Psalm 103: 1–2

Vespers
> permeating
> impacting
> influencing
> transforming
>> the visible
>> and invisible universe
>>> past and present

Bless the Lord, O my soul, and all within me,
His holy name.

The nations shall fear the name of the Lord and all the
Earth's kings Your glory.
When the Lord shall build up Zion again,
And appear resplendent in glory.
The Lord will turn to the prayers of the helpless;
And will not despise their prayers.

Psalm 102: 16–18

Surrending at compline
   a form of prayer
      accessible to us
         even when prayer seems
            empty of meaning
         even when we have forgotten
          how to pray

You, O Lord, are enthroned forever,
and Your renown is from age to age.

O Lord, Your strength gives joy to the king,
how Your saving help makes him glad!
You have granted him my heart's desire,
You have not refused the prayer of my lips.
You have granted your blessings to him forever.
You have made him rejoice with the joy of Your presence.

Psalm 21: 2, 7

Matins
> open
> receptive to the
> limitless
> boundless
>> unconditional love of God

O Lord, arise in Your strength;
we shall sing and praise Your power.

They are happy, who dwell in Your house,
forever singing Your praise.
They are happy, whose strength is in You,
in whose hearts are the roads to Zion.
They walk with ever growing strength,
they will see the God of gods in Zion.

Psalm 84: 5-6, 8

Rating ourselves
wanting ourselves to be different
    never brings happiness

Happiness is ours
    When we wholeheartedly unconditionally accept
        the person we are
            this day

How lovely is Your dwelling place,
O Lord of hosts.

You make springs gush forth in the valleys;
they flow in between the hills.
On their banks dwell the birds of Heaven;
from the branches they sing their song.

From your dwelling You water the hills;
Earth drinks its fill of Your gift.
You make the grass grow for the cattle,
and the plants to serve our needs.

Psalm 104: 10, 12, 13-14

Creation
  reflected upon
  prayed over
    listened to
      leads to gratitude
        discovering
        a new strength
          within us
            calling us to new depths
            each day

In You, O Lord, I place my total trust.

You have prepared a banquet for me
in the sight of my foes.
My head You have anointed with oil;
my cup is overflowing.
Surely goodness and kindness shall follow me
all the days of my life.
In the Lord's own house shall I dwell
forever and ever.

Psalm 23: 5–6

O Source of life
   the more we gather
         store
         hoard
         put away
               the less we receive
the more we
         share
         let go
         give away
               the more we receive
It is in giving we receive

The Lord is my shepherd;
there is nothing I shall want.

I will praise You, Lord, my God, with all my heart
And glorify your name forever.
For Your love for me has been great;
You have saved me from the depths of the grave.
You, God of mercy and compassion,
slow to anger, O Lord,
abounding in love and truth,
turn and take pity on me.

Psalm 86: 12–13, 15-16

Conscious living
    knowing
        inner freedom
    working
        with dignity
        without enslavement
Free
    to take up work
        to put it down
    to give thanks and praise
        when the bell rings
            for sext at midday

I will praise You, Lord my God, with all my heart
and glorify Your name forever.

Alleluia!
My soul, give praise to the Lord;
I will praise the Lord all my days,
make music to my God while I live.

They are happy who are helped by Jacob's God,
whose hope is in the Lord their God,
who alone made Heaven and Earth,
the seas and all they contain.

Psalm 146: 1–2, 5-6

Mid-afternoon
    shadows gathering
        - a symbol of death

Nones
    praying
        for a holy death
            a completion of life
            a celebration of life

The Lord is kind and full of compassion.

To You, Lord God, my eyes are turned;
in You I take refuge; spare my soul!
From the trap they have laid for me keep me safe;
keep me from the snares of those who do evil.

Psalm 141: 8–9

Accepting the mystery of our being
accepting ourselves unconditionally
not having to prove anything
we become
the self we were born to be

Hear my voice when I cry to You, O Lord.

The Lord will not abandon His people,
nor forsake His chosen heritage.
When I think: "I have lost my foothold,"
Your mercy, Lord, holds me up.
When cares increase in my heart,
Your consolation calms my soul.

Psalm 94: 14, 18–19

Compline
  drawing us into
      the movement of night
  assisting us
      to acknowledge the greatness of God
          as the sky changes
              and night falls

God will be the rock where I take refuge.

To You, O Lord I lift up my soul.
My God, I trust You, let me not be disappointed,
Lord make me know Your ways.
Lord teach me Your paths.
Make me walk in Your truth, and teach me,
for You are God my saviour.

Psalm 25: 1, 4-5

Tuning into ourselves
    an invitation to listen
        to silence
        to stillness
            to God
                enabling us to be
                    more receptive
                    more understanding
                    more fruitful
                        as night gives way to day

All the Lord's paths are mercy and faithfulness.

It is good to give thanks to the Lord,
to make music to Your name O most high
to proclaim Your love in the morning,
and Your truth in the watches of the night,
on the ten stringed lyre and the lute ,
with the murmuring sound of the harp.

Psalm 92: 1-4

Early in the morning
 the music of gratitude
  rises easily in our heart
   when we remember
    the many gifts
    graces
    chances
     we have been given
 the music of gratitude
  available
   all day
   everyday
    when we remember

Your deeds, O Lord, have made me glad.

Turn Your ear O Lord and give answer,
for I am poor and needy.
Preserve my life, for I am faithful;
save the servant who trust in You.
You are my God, have mercy on me O Lord,
for I cry to You all day long.
Give joy to Your servant O Lord,
for to You I lift up my soul.

Psalm 86: 1–4

Prime calling us
    to the daily task of work
Calling us in our poverty and riches
    to make our world
        a better place
    a call in history
    a vocation in time
        to remake
        reshape
        co create
        our world

To You, O Lord, I lift up my soul.

Lord, let my cry come before You:
teach me by Your word.
Let my pleading come before You:
save me by Your promise.
Let Your hand be ready to help me,
since I have chosen Your precepts.

Psalm 119: 169–170, 173

Terce

Emptying our mind
emptying our heart
creating
space for
peace
serenity
kindness
space for
listening
learning
knowing
as the hollow empty reed
leaves space for music

Teach me good judgment and knowledge,
for I trust in Your commands.

The Lord is good and upright,
Showing the path to those who stray.
Guiding the humble in the right path,
and teaching the way to the poor.

Pslam 25: 8–9

Negativity
> unacknowledged
> unresolved is
>> crippling, controlling

Negativity
> faced
> named
> claimed
>> brings
>> awareness
>> peace
>> integrity
>> dignity
>> freedom
>> truth
>> happiness

Remember Your mercy, Lord,
and the love You have shown from of old.

Come and hear, all who fear God,
I will tell what God did for my soul.
To God I cried aloud,
with high praise ready on my tongue.

Psalm 66: 16–17

All is gift
    everything
        a unique expression of God's heart

Acknowledged
    named
    claimed
        we give thanks and praise

Blest be God, who did not reject my prayer.

This is my prayer to You,
my prayer for Your favour.
In Your great love, answer me, O God,
with Your help that never fails.
Do not hide Your face from Your servant;
answer quickly for I am in distress.

Psalm 69: 14, 18

Seeking God's help

with confidence

with sure hope

knowing we are heard

accepting with gratitude

what is sent

a prayer

of petition

of gratitude

bringing peace

Come close to my soul and redeem me.

The Lord will bless those who fear Him,
the little no less than the great.
To you may the Lord grant increase,
to you and all your children.
May you be blessed by the Lord,
The maker of Heaven and Earth.
The Heavens belong to the Lord,
but to us God has given the Earth.

Psalm 115: 13–16

Fear without awareness
destructive
crippling

Fear with awareness
acknowledged
accepted
honoured
a way to inner peace

The Lord remembers us, and He will bless us.

O where can I go from Your spirit,
or where can I flee from Your face?
If I climb the Heavens You are there.
If I lie in the grave, You are there.
If I take the wings of the dawn
and dwell at the seas furthest end,
even there Your hand would lead me,
Your right hand would hold me fast.

Psalm 139: 7-10

Stillness and silence
  awaits us
    everywhere
  we find it
    when we stop
    to wonder
    to notice
      the cloud over the moon
      the changing sky
      the sight of the dim light appearing on the horizon
      the first hint of morning chorus
        the countless wonders of day and night

O Lord, You search me and You know me.

Planted in the house of the Lord,
they will flourish in the courts of our God,
still bearing fruit when they are old,
still full of sap, still green,
to proclaim that the Lord is just.
My rock, in whom there is no wrong.

Psalm 92: 14–16

We arise today
    like the morning sun
        feeling safe
        protected
        watched over
        cared for

we arise today
    with courage
        to ascend beyond the fray
          regardless of difficulties
        knowing
          nothing can destroy
          the gift of who we are

You have gladdened me, O Lord, by Your deeds.

May the glory of the Lord last for ever!
May the Lord rejoice in creation!
God looks on the Earth and it trembles;
at God's touch, the mountains send forth smoke.
I will sing to the Lord all my life,
make music to my God while I live.

Psalm 104: 31–33

Prime

    The demands

            of life

            of work

Challenging us to

            embrace our creaturehood

            discover our heart's core

            befriend our inner wisdom

            recognise the music within

            rejoicing in creations story

I will rejoice in the Lord.

Lord, You have been good to your servant
according to Your word.
Teach me discernment and knowledge,
for I trust in Your commands.
You are good and Your deeds are good;
teach me Your statutes.

Psalm 119: 65-66, 68

Facing the vulnerability of our humanness
    the bedrock of truth
Accepting the fragility of our humanness
    the way of truth
Reverencing the brokenness of our humanness
    the mystery of truth

O Lord, Your merciful love fills the Earth.

God's ways are steadfastness and truth
for those faithful to the covenant decrees.

Those who revere the Lord
will be shown the path they should choose.
Their souls will live in happiness
and their children shall possess the land.

Psalm 25: 10, 12–13

Feeling unloved
  unacknowledged
  undervalued
      we find it hard to love
  realising we are loved unconditionally
          accepting ourselves as we are
              healed
              we love anew

In Your merciful love remember me, because of
Your goodness, O Lord.

Alleluia!
God covers the Heavens with clouds,
and prepares the rain for the Earth,
making mountains sprout with grass,
and with plants to serve our needs,
God provides the beasts with their food,
and the young ravens when they cry.

Psalm 147: 8-9

Each day
    a unique gift given
Nones
    giving thanks
        for all that we have
        for all that is
            given
            received
            taken;
                gifts of the day

My soul, give praise to the Lord.

Wisdom is bright and does not grow dim;
by those who love her she is readily seen,
and found by those who look for her.
Quick to anticipate those who desire her, she
makes herself known to them.

Wisdom 6: 12–14

In the evening of our
    day
    in saying yes
        accepting
        embracing
        the day
      we begin to discover
          who we are
            wisdom awakens
            we give thanks

Wisdom is found by those who look for her.

Alleluia!
Tremble, O Earth, before the Lord,
in the presence of the God of Jacob,
who turns the rock into a pool
and flint into a spring of water.

Psalm 114: 7–8

Giving thanks
  a step towards self-acceptance

Accepting self
  we learn to love ourselves

Loving ourselves
  we are healed

Not us, O Lord, but to Your name give the glory.

I am sure I shall see the Lord's goodness
in the land of the living.
In the Lord, hold firm and take heart.
Hope in the Lord!

Psalm 27: 13-14

Wisdom waiting to be found
    waiting for us
        to listen
        to accept
        to discover
            in stillness
            in silence
                the wonder of who we are
                the wonder of our being

Instruct me, Lord, in Your way.

The Lord's voice resounding on the waters,
the Lord on immensity of waters;
the voice of the Lord, full of power,
the voice of the Lord, full of splendour.

Psalm 29: 3–4

Morning
  blessing us
    with time and space
        to be attentive
              to all that is new
  blessing us
    with time and space to
          look
          listen
          see
          hear
                become aware
                    this new day
  blessing us
    with time and space
          to experience the wonder
          as sunlight

The Lord will give strength to His people, the Lord
will bless His people with peace.

Give thanks, and acclaim God's name.
Make known God's deeds among the peoples.
Consider the Lord, who is strong;
constantly seek His face.
Remember the wonders of the Lord,
the miracles and judgements pronounced.

Psalm 105: 1, 4–5

Our unawakened mind
　seeking happiness
　　　searching
　　　grasping
　　　　　restless
　　　　　not satisfied
　　　　　lost.
Our awakened mind
　seeking happiness
　　　stops
　　　reflects
　　　ponders
　　　knows
　　　　　happiness is here
　　　　　happiness is now

It is Your face, O Lord, that I seek.

They are happy whose life is blameless,
who follow God's law!
They are happy who do God's will,
seeking God with all their hearts.
Who never do anything evil,
but walk in God's ways.

Psalm 119: 1–3

Terce
  stopping to pray
  seeing no borders
  no boundaries
  letting go of divisions
          opening to difference
          opening to diversity
  seeing beauty in everyone, in everything
          all around us
          in diversity
          in unity

Teach me to walk in Your ways.

The mountains melt like wax
before the Lord all the Earth.
The skies proclaim God's justice;
all peoples see God's glory.
Let those who serve idols be ashamed,
those who boast of their worthless gods.
All you spirits, worship the Lord.

Psalm 97: 5-7

Creation
  always becoming
      never complete
  always being shaped
      never static
  always evolving
      we are co-creators
  shaping
  moulding
  fashioning
  remaking creation
      all day
      every day

Light shines forth for the just one,
and joy for the upright of heart.

I rejoiced when I heard them say:
"Let us go to God's house."
And now our feet are standing
within your gates, O Jerusalem.
Jerusalem is built as a city strongly compact.
It is there that the tribes go up,
the tribes of the Lord.

Psalm 122: 1–4

Afternoon
being grateful
rejoicing in life
being grateful
increasing awareness
removing limits
the ordinary
becomes extraordinary
being grateful
renewed
living with joy
living to the full

For the sake of my family and friends, let me say,
"Peace upon You."

Redeem me from those who oppress me
and I will keep Your precepts.
Let Your face shine on your servant,
and teach me Your decrees.
Tears stream from my eyes,
because Your law is disobeyed.

Psalm 119: 134–136

Truth comes
in pairs of opposites:
we are strong
when we embrace our weaknesses
we are teachers
when we can be taught
we enjoy others
when we enjoy ourselves
we are wise
when we accept our own foolishness
we find true laughter
when we laugh at ourselves

Let my steps be guided by Your promise;
may evil never rule me.

Alleluia!
I love the Lord, for the Lord has heard
the cry of my appeal.
The Lord was attentive to me
in the day when I called.

Psalm 116: 1–2

Accepting our woundedness
  releases energy
    a healing power
      for ourselves
      others
      the universe

I will walk in the presence of the Lord.

Those who dwell in the shelter of the most high
and abide in the shade of the Almighty,
Say to the Lord, "my refuge,
my stronghold, my God in whom I trust!"

Psalm 91: 1-2

Matins

opening to our senses

sight

hearing

touch

smell

taste

the wonder of this moment

the wonder of our being

opening to what is now

the wonder of God

You will not fear the terror of the night,
nor the arrow that flies by day.

Happy indeed are those
who follow not the council of the wicked.
They are like the tree that is planted
beside the flowing waters,
that yields its fruit in due season,
and whose leaves will never fade,
and all they do shall prosper.

Psalm 1: 1, 3

Like a tree
  planted in good soil
      by flowing waters
        we too
          rooted in love
            yield fruit
              drawing sustenance
                from the source of all life
                  in due season

Happy are those whose delight
is in the law of the Lord.

You have given me a short span of days;
my life is as nothing in your sight.
A mere breath, the one who stood so firm;
A mere shadow, the one who passes by;
A mere breath, the hoarded riches,
and who will take them, no one knows.
In You rests all my hope.

Psalm 39: 6-8

Prime
  challenging us
    to be fully present
      in life
        wherever we are
          now

Tomorrow
  the enemy of today
    we cannot be tomorrow
      what we can be today

Surely all mankind stands as but a breath.

But You, Lord, are a shield about me,
my glory, who lift up my head.
I cry aloud to You, Lord.
You answer from Your holy mountain.
O Lord of salvation, bless Your people!

Psalm 3: 4–7, 9

Faith

    waiting

        with promise

        in a time of darkness

        and uncertainty

Faith

    gentle strength

        in adversity

I lie down, I sleep and I wake,
for the Lord upholds me.

How gracious is the Lord, and just;
our God has compassion.
The Lord protects the simple hearts;
I was helpless so God saved me.
I will walk in the presence of the Lord
in the land of the living.

Psalm 116A: 5–6, 9

Sext
    fallow time
        rest time
Rest-time
    bringing
        vigour
        nourishment
        renewal
        openness
    bringing
        readiness
            to listen
            to respond
            to the inner voice

He has kept my soul from death, my eyes from tears, and my feet from stumbling.

Come to me Lord with Your help,
that I may see the joy of Your chosen ones ,
and may rejoice in the gladness of Your nation,
and share the glory of Your people.

Psalm 106: 4–5

Sext
A time to give thanks
   for our gifts
      the gifts of other
A time to experience the joy
   That gratitude brings

O give thanks to the Lord who is good,
whose love endures forever.

Let the family of Israel say,
"God's love endures for ever."
Let the family of Aaron say,
"God's love endures for ever."
Let those who fear the Lord say,
"God's love endures for ever."

Psalm 118: 2-4

Listening to the small voice within
in ways that let us hear and
discover the person we are called to be
in our being
in our doing
in our delightful uniqueness

The Lord is at my side; I do not fear.

But You, O Lord, how long?
Return, Lord, rescue my soul.
Save me in Your merciful love.
For the Lord has heard my weeping.
The Lord has heard my plea,
the Lord will accept my prayer.

Psalm 6: 4–5, 9

Living in the present
   acknowledging the divine presence everywhere
      always here and now
   helps us greet the night
      with gratitude
   helps us welcome death
      when its moment comes.

Have mercy on me, Lord.

Awakening Inner Peace